POI TOWERS

CREATIVE STARS

EDITED BY DAISY JOB

First published in Great Britain in 2023 by:

 Young**Writers**® ── Est. 1991 ─

Young Writers
Remus House
Coltsfoot Drive
Peterborough
PE2 9BF
Telephone: 01733 890066
Website: www.youngwriters.co.uk

Printed and bound in the UK by BookPrintingUK
Website: www.bookprintinguk.com
YB0558I

FOREWORD

For Young Writers' latest competition we invited primary school pupils to enroll at a new school, Poetry Towers, where they could let their imaginations roam free.

At Poetry Towers the timetable of subjects on offer is unlimited, so pupils could choose any topic that inspired them and write in any poetry style. We provided free resources including lesson plans, poetry guides and inspiration and examples to help pupils craft a piece of writing they can be proud of.

Here at Young Writers our aim is to encourage creativity in children and to inspire a love of the written word, so it's great to get such an amazing response, with some absolutely fantastic poems. It's important for children to express themselves and a great way to engage them is to allow them to write about what they care about. The result is a varied collection of poems with a range of styles and techniques that showcase their creativity and writing ability.

We'd like to congratulate all the young poets in this anthology, the latest alumni of the Young Writers' academy of poetry and rhyme. We hope this inspires them to continue with their creative writing.

CONTENTS

Abbey Primary School, Morden

Zoya Khalid (10)	1
Aganya Mukunthan (10)	2
Katerin Carrillo Lema (10)	3
Summer May Dutfield (10)	4
Daria Datkun (10)	5
Karis Duggan (10)	6
Malaikah Noor (10)	7
Liam Morris (9)	8
Arshia Vaid (10)	9
Filip Chojniak (10)	10
Emily Gibb (10)	11
Max Rea (10)	12
Masroor Janjua (10)	13
Sophie Ersapah (10)	14
Lora Marian Markov (10)	15
Rishan Robinson (10)	16
Shritoban Mukherjee (9)	17
Savannah Angel Jessey (9)	18

Bersted Green Primary School, Bognor Regis

Athena Mayer (10)	19
Alesha Begum (10)	20
Harry Grainger (9)	21
Lena Makowska (11)	22

Curwen Primary School, Plaistow

Olanna Ogedengbe (8)	23
Phoebe-Grace Olayinka (9)	24
Sarrinah Zaman (10)	26
Delisa Kabir (8)	28
Heather Macalintal (11)	30

Ibrahim Rahman (9)	31
Rufaida Roha (11)	32
Leah Bamotra (9)	33
Nushraalam Subha (10)	34
Selena Hyder (8)	35
Claire Liu (7)	36
Courtney Wynter (11)	37
Bethel Adeniran (8)	38
Jasmine Peasah (8)	39
Tahfeem Toshana (7)	40
Humaira Harris (7)	41
Raed Samee (10)	42
Kristabel Kuagbela (8)	43
Abiegail Jimenez (7)	44
Huryra Chowdhury (9)	45
Ibrahim Hussain (8)	46
Amara Khan (8)	47
Anushka Dhir (10)	48
Clarissa Jones (8)	49
Laila Bouchaib (10)	50
Brey Rimando (8)	51
Benji Nicholls (8)	52
Khaleesi Jones-Desilva (8)	53
Danica Yesan (9)	54
Diego Bernardino Alves Dos Santos (10)	55
Ismail Miah (7)	56

Farington Primary School, Farington

Georgia Palin (9)	57
Zahra Randall (10)	58
Riley Unitt (10)	60
Lucy Broadhurst (9)	62
Darcie Bilsborough (9)	63

Sonny Benson (10)	64
Nathan Morement (10)	66
Lola Masterman (10)	67
Jake Harbour (9)	68
Michael Haynes (10)	69
Nadia Struska (10)	70

Ponsbourne St Mary's CE Primary School, Hertford

Pantelina Cappalonga (9)	71
Marina Louca (8)	72
Anthony Jordan (9)	73
Berri-Rae Pryor (9)	74
Anastasia Tsekouras (8)	75
Gabriella Delfino (7)	76
Alexander Papaleontiou (8)	77
Naomi Lilley (7)	78
Evie Spafford (9)	79

Send CE Primary School, Send

Maia Cooper (11)	80
Kai Cooper (9)	82
Betsy Anscombe (8)	84
Azaan Afsar (10)	85
Betsy Stevens (10)	86
Eyleen Marcel (10)	87
Helena Collins (8)	88
Florence Booth (9)	89
Eliza Attwater (8)	90
Ava-Rose Downey (10)	91
Tomasina Gallagher (9)	92
Megan Biddles (8)	93
Indira Wilkinson (9)	94
Chlea Marcel (7)	95
Lucy Middleton (7)	96
Scout Marshall (10)	97
Eve Ellis (9)	98
Madison Poley (10)	99
Amelie Rogers (9)	100
Poppy Banks (7)	101
Jessica Woods (8)	102
Mia Drummond (8)	103

Mali Reuben (8)	104
Sienna Stafford (7)	105
Ada Reuben (8)	106
Flora Bricklebank (10)	107
Jessica Simmons (7)	108
Emily Harrison (9)	109
Ben Warne (9)	110

St Matthew's Primary School, Luton

Jessica O'Reilly (10)	111
Kuba Dąbrowski (11)	112
Huzaifa Malik (11)	114
Ioana Supuran (11)	116
Tallulah Kingham (11)	118
Roland Takacs (11)	120
Ginelle Ofosu-Appiah (11)	122
Tia-Marie Stewart (11)	124
Zuzanna Manuszewska (10)	126
Sunaina Ayesha (11)	128
Fjorela Kasa (10)	130
Zuzanna Janko (10)	132
Ameer Ali (11)	134
Ismail Hogan (11)	136
Taylor Gardner (11)	138
Witek Pelka (10)	140
Tyrese Turner (11)	142
Ethan Mlambo (11)	144
Marcel Mieszkowski (10)	145
Marilia Maxhari (11)	146
Jaydon West (11)	147
Zakariyya Malik (10)	148
Natalia Wroblewska (11)	149
Rebecca Grab (10)	150
Aleksandra Janewa (11)	151
Abdur-Rahman Brora (11)	152
Ferdous Kabiri (11)	153
Grace Yanju (10)	154
Kamila Kotlinska (10)	155
Malaika Lodhi (11)	156
Ada Gubas (11)	157
Keelan Devlin (11)	158
Fazal Waseem (10)	159

Arabella McIntyre (11)	160
Ricardo Nambam Sanha (10)	161
Aleesa Afzal (10)	162
Deken Walsh (10)	163
Dannah Sunish (11)	164
Rehan Syed (11)	165
Zofia Sabiniarz (10)	166
Jadesola Adeshina (11)	167
Bradley Siluba (11)	168
Szymon Chris Sniec (11)	169
Destiny-Marie Fowler (11)	170
Amelia Rowley (10)	171
Siyana Sultana (10)	172
Julia Gluzinska (10)	173
Athil Ali (11)	174
Bartosz Smielecki (11)	175
Enrika Mihada (11)	176
Nathaniel Mwanza (11)	177
Elle Yit (11)	178
Siele Antanaviciute (11)	179
Deenah Halimi (10)	180
Chloe Mcguiness (10)	181
Joseph Oche Igoche (11)	182
Dwight Acquah (11)	183
Zuzanna Nawvocka (11)	184
Medeea Droga (11)	185
Khalid Atunrase (11)	186
Gabriel Kotecki (11)	187
Nikola Banach (10)	188
Kacper Falkowski (11)	189
Ava Jaklik-Street (11)	190
Oluwatomisin Taiwo (10)	191
Denis Leleu (11)	192
Conor Morsley-Gavin (11)	193
Ziqi Liu (11)	194
Tazrian Ahmed (11)	195
Owen Brackstone (11)	196
Irfan Ahmed (11)	197
Keivin Hasaj (11)	198
Sahil Miah (10)	199
Julia Dabrowksa (11)	200
Beatrix Kerekes (11)	201
Kamil Babusa (11)	202

Scarlett Maccow (10)	203
Maame Afia (10)	204

Stanton Community Primary School, Stanton

Annalise Sharpe (10)	205
Seren Olney (11)	206
Abigail Mayes (11)	207
Holly Maudlin-Moss (9)	208
Isabelle Steed (8)	209
Summer Pickup (9)	210
Henry Wright (8)	211
Esmie O'Reilly (10)	212
Harry Shaw (8)	213
Caitlin Goodridge (8)	214

Woodlands Primary School, Linwood

Shaun Keziah Massengo Fleary (12)	215
Anna Maria Reo (12)	216
Teigan Reid (12)	217

THE POEMS

The Enchanted Forest

Deep in the hidden forest, where all magic begins,
Lies mysterious secrets, and its adventure spins.
There are fairies, who all marvellously glitter,
And all the gnomes proudly jitter.

The trees dance, and the flowers sing,
Orchids whisper secrets as they sway in spring.
The delicate and dear dandelions glow,
Alongside the pretty and radiant roses below.

Illuminating like a fiery ball rests the sun,
Which smiles in utmost excitement and fun.
Remember to keep this a secret and remain silent,
As something may lurk that's dangerous and
violent...

Zoya Khalid (10)
Abbey Primary School, Morden

What Could This Mean?

The room fills with darkness,
Not a ray of light can be seen,
Souls dancing to a dark tune,
What could this mean?

Candles twirl in the moonlight,
Bats fly like shooting stars, *whoosh!*
This isn't right,
What could this mean?

Cats which are black hiss at you,
With their menacing teeth,
Don't touch them or you will be their next meal,
You don't know their deal,
What could this mean?

Crash!

Dark. Eerie. Perilous.

Aganya Mukunthan (10)
Abbey Primary School, Morden

Father's Day

Oh no! Today is Father's Day!
What am I gonna do?
Me and Mother all forgot,
What are we gonna do?
A gift to keep you working,
A present to help you cook,
A gadget for your pencil case,
No, that would just be rude,
Let's wrap it,
Let's tie it,
And don't take a peek,
Dad, don't be impatient,
Your time will soon begin,
Here it is, Dad,
In bed you should stay,
Everything you should have is love and cake,
Since today is your special day.

Katerin Carrillo Lema (10)
Abbey Primary School, Morden

What's Your Favourite Animal?

What's your favourite animal?
Mine's a kangaroo,
Look, it's stuck in sticky goo!
What's your favourite animal?
Mine's a cat,
Look, it's scratching a mat!
What's your favourite animal?
Mine's a dog,
Look, it's chasing a frog!
What's your favourite animal?
Mine's a mouse,
Look, it's going in my house!
What's your favourite animal?
Mine's a fox,
Look, it's in a box!

Summer May Dutfield (10)
Abbey Primary School, Morden

The Road Trip

"We're going on holiday! We're going on a plane!"
Screamed May, who was cuddling her teddy all
ready to play.
I took out my phone and was texting my friend.
'Life is a spinning carousel with lots of mixed
events
And who knows, they might never end', she said...
I gazed out the window and realised she was right.
Life is a holiday, I thought
And nothing will stop our delight.

Daria Datkun (10)
Abbey Primary School, Morden

The Furry Fire Fox

This fox roamed the land,
Sparks playing like a band.
Warmth and love spread,
The fire lit up the night as he lay in his bed.

His paws lit up the ground,
As he howled like a hound.
Smoke twirled off his ears,
As he never shed any tears.

Everyone loved his red, fiery fur,
And many people loved his little pur.
This is the creature that roamed the lands,
Never to be found.

Karis Duggan (10)
Abbey Primary School, Morden

Backpack

I've got a new backpack
Which is so pretty
The first day of school
The whole school made fun of it (even teachers)
This made me feel embarrassed
The next day I got a different bag (which I didn't like)
So this time half of the school made fun of it
This made me feel sad
After that day I had an ugly bag
But this time no one made a peep out of their mouth
This made me feel relief!

Malaikah Noor (10)
Abbey Primary School, Morden

The Game Called Football

The cheers and tears of the game called football
Where teams and regions battle for the best of the
season
The GOATs become the greats
Pelé, Messi, these are the people nobody hates
The gods of football inspire the people
That give out fliers, power shots
The tap-in rockers and the bicycle kick shockers
That is the story of the game called football.

Liam Morris (9)
Abbey Primary School, Morden

Family Life

Family life is what I want,
Family life is what I need.
I can't live without it and
I can't live without my family
So this is what I need.
We get our knowledge from them.
We get our love from them.
Who is your favourite family member?
Mine is Dad!
Who is your favourite?
Mine is Mum!
Who is your favourite family member?

Arshia Vaid (10)
Abbey Primary School, Morden

A Poem About Poems

I love poems
I can do whatever I want
I can be free
Until my pencil goes blunt
I can have fun
All day
I can do something crazy
And nobody will say
You can't do that
I can do
Acrostic, riddle, rhyme
I do this whenever I have time
I sing my poems
All day
And when it's over
I go and play.

Filip Chojniak (10)
Abbey Primary School, Morden

World Crisis

Our feet as cold as ice,
Our hearts have turned blue,
What was once green, is now black as ash.
We're cutting down trees, and that's sooo fun.
The world crisis has not even begun.
People are starving while we're sitting here,
Laughing at TV and sipping on beer.
Smash! Crash! Bash!
Will we survive?

Emily Gibb (10)
Abbey Primary School, Morden

The Best Sport

Sports, sport, we all love sports,
We will never stop loving football.
Rugby, football, tennis, basketball, there is so much to choose from,
Messi or Ronaldo, Pelé or Roberto Carlos, who is the best?
Who will win the next World Cup?
Will there be a next GOAT playing for Argentina following in Messi's football footsteps?

Max Rea (10)

Abbey Primary School, Morden

Always Football

8 o'clock already,
Running like a cheetah.
Pressing the buttons fast and steady,
Manchester United vs Manchester City.

The TV is a box full of ants,
Rashford nutmegs, dribbling...
Goal! Manchester City fans, no buts or can'ts,
Just in the nick of time, full-time!

Masroor Janjua (10)
Abbey Primary School, Morden

Besties

When I was little
I liked to play
With my besties
In every way
Sports, role plays and board games
I even liked to lay
I liked to read with them
When we met each other we'd say
"Hey!"
Then we'd go pay
To go get snacks and sweets.

Sophie Ersapah (10)
Abbey Primary School, Morden

My Normal School Day

When I get into school,
Someone acts like a fool,
Boys end up daydreaming,
And one girl keeps screaming!
Maths gets worse,
A girl is casting a curse,
Someone keeps on crying,
There's a lie that the teacher is buying...

Lora Marian Markov (10)
Abbey Primary School, Morden

Strange Animals

Animals, animals, animals
Strange animals
Animals can be cool
Some could look like a fool.

Imagine living with every animal
Chaotic, right?
This is an absolute nightmare
Think about where they would sleep at night.

Rishan Robinson (10)
Abbey Primary School, Morden

Football: The Best Sport

Football: the best sport,
A fun game with a ball,
It's popular and competitive,
It's played wherever you live,
Kicking a ball could not be more fun,
Football: the beautiful game.

Shritoban Mukherjee (9)
Abbey Primary School, Morden

BFFs

Friends are basically your life,
If you don't have a friend, well...
Anyway, best friends are amazing,
They're like your family,
I'm joking but it feels like it.

Savannah Angel Jessey (9)
Abbey Primary School, Morden

Nature

Nature rules, plastic drools,
Plastic invades whilst nature is struggling to
remain,
Animals survive on what's left alive,
Nature is alive whilst plastic is not fantastic,
Plastic floats by boats,
Sea creatures die from plastic which is washed up
onto the ocean bay,
Animals die upon the bay more than once a day,
More and more, why do they do this?
Barely anyone trying to stop this
Why? Why? Why? I ask
Pollution is not the solution
It wouldn't hurt to pick up a piece or more of
plastic
And put it in the bin so we can have a clean
environment to live in
So listen to this and think about it
Or maybe act straight away.

Athena Mayer (10)
Bersted Green Primary School, Bognor Regis

The Trinity

God is the Father,
God is the Son,
God is The Holy Spirit,
God is One.

Father, Father in the air,
Father, Father everywhere,
Father will stay with you,
Father will keep you safe.
Father gave you The Son.

The Son was Jesus Christ,
The Son was sacrificed,
The Son was killed,
The Son died,
The Son was memorised.

The Holy Spirit will guide you here,
The Holy Spirit will always be near,
The Holy Spirit will be in you,
The Holy Spirit will stay with you.

Alesha Begum (10)
Bersted Green Primary School, Bognor Regis

The Pollution Problem

Whilst walking on the shore one day
Litter I saw on Wales' bay
Why did they do this to the island?
I saw
Plastic bags moving like jellyfish, a tower of rusting
cans
Animals getting tangled and banged
A half-full bottle full of shame
Lost boxes, ice cream cones, McDonald's Happy
Meals,
Why are humans doing this to the world?

Harry Grainger (9)
Bersted Green Primary School, Bognor Regis

Poems And Music

A poem is like a song without music
But when you read it out loud
It's like singing without music
But when you add music
It's a song.
But a poem's not a song,
It's a short story or sentence.

Lena Makowska (11)
Bersted Green Primary School, Bognor Regis

My Life

Maybe my life isn't always easy
But I love living it anyway
I have a family who are always there for me
They love me no matter what I do or say

I have friends to talk and make fun with
They pick me up when I'm down
Make me see true friendship is not a myth
They cheer me up and never let me down

I have strength and my courage too
My pride, loving heart and loyalty
Whatever may happen, I will get through
And I will enjoy life fully

I have so many things to be grateful for around me
So many things that make me smile and laugh
My life doesn't need to be perfect
Everyone makes mistakes
And I love my life the way it is
Now I enjoy it.

Olanna Ogedengbe (8)
Curwen Primary School, Plaistow

Lifelong Questions

My dad has a wife to continue his life.
Life, wait, what about my life?
Is it bad? Am I mad or sad?
Can I drive a car or go to a bar?
All these questions...
Phoebe, pay attention!
I follow the rules,
Listen to the fools,
But haven't had an answer to my lifelong wonder.
My mum has a husband who is strong and hardly wrong.
She continues her life.
Life, wait, what about my life?
"Strive for success," teachers say
They act like they do every single day.
Can I ask questions that are personal?
Or stay in that tiny bubble?
My head to my toes grows and grows.
Calm down, don't let them tear you down.
The haters are bullies,
We are peaceful trees.

Sometimes life is hard
And we want to make a little card.
When you think about it
Love is as simple and rare as a white dove.
I'm only nine and my life is perfectly fine.
"Be resilient," teachers say
But hey, we're just having one of those days.
My lifelong questions.

Phoebe-Grace Olayinka (9)

Curwen Primary School, Plaistow

My Victorian Nightmare

I'm a workhouse girl
Danger, danger
Beware the master
Greed and selfish
Spiteful, vindictive
His whip grins as it slaps my cheek
I would much rather be on a mountain peak
I need help, I'm hungry... Save me!

I'm as poor as a stray
I'm as dirty as a puddle
The machines make me dirtier
Chewing on high level
The wheel cuts me
Tries to slice me in half
Needles pierce me through the air
Pinching and piercing everywhere

I'm as skinny as a toothpick
I'm as filthy as mud
I feel like I'm burning in a fire blaze
But I go through and try to extinguish the flame

Sometimes I dislike fixing machines
It doesn't really match my idea of daily routines

But...

I keep fighting, fighting for my rights
Trying to make my way into the spotlight
Talking about the freedom we deserve
Until we become serene and peaceful like a gliding
bird.

Sarrinah Zaman (10)
Curwen Primary School, Plaistow

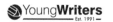

You Are Unique In Many Different Ways

I have a sad cloud over my head
With the crowd following me everywhere I go.
The way they were bullying me was emptying all
the joy out of me.
In class I looked at the time for the lesson to end,
I felt like a lime, sad and slimy, slouching on my
chair.

Once every hour passed, more and more people
came picking on me,
In lessons, break time and even home times.
I couldn't take it, I was livid.
I thought this would be the end, no matter how
hard I tried to blend in,
I'm always the odd one out with no friend.

I didn't want to go there anymore.
So I gave up holding my tears, trying to blend in
And trying not to hear those bad comments.
I felt sad and bad about myself,

The moments I had in this school were not happy
or good.
I thought, you shouldn't care what others think of
you,
You are unique, everyone's unique in every way
And you are special too.

Delisa Kabir (8)
Curwen Primary School, Plaistow

Goodbye

Ciao, adios, goodbye.
The time is here, please don't cry!
Save your tears as we wave to you,
As we start again, somewhere new.

Others beginning to stress,
Many finding it a time to rest.
The moment is going to be very soon,
To begin spreading our wings out of the cocoon.

As we laughed and cried each day,
There were no feelings of dismay.
I hope for it just to be the same,
Where nothing changed since this day came.

Next year, we'll be working hard and making you
proud!
Doing our best like we vowed,
And with more memories and moments to come,
Goodbye.

Heather Macalintal (11)
Curwen Primary School, Plaistow

30

End The Pollution

Pollution, pollution,
There has to be a solution,
Now we need a new revolution,
People are crying,
Children are dying,
The world will be ending,
If we don't start mending,
So let's stop pretending,
And start defending
This beautiful Earth
That we have seen since birth.

Pollution, pollution, pollution,
We have a cure to the solution,
Let's all pull together and make a change,
By reducing, reusing and recycling,
We could be mending,
This Earth we might be ending,
Pollution, pollution, pollution,
We now have the solution.

Ibrahim Rahman (9)
Curwen Primary School, Plaistow

All About Friendship

Friendship is a precious gift
That makes our lives more bright
It's the bond that we share with others
Who support us day and night

Friendship is a source of joy
That fills our hearts with love
It's the feeling that we belong
To a circle we are part of

Friendship is a treasure chest
That holds our memories dear
It's the place we can find
The stories we love

Friendship is a golden thread
That connects us through and through
It's the thing that makes us strong
When we have friends like you.

Rufaida Roha (11)
Curwen Primary School, Plaistow

God's Plan

I once had a dream I could fly up high
In the never-ending blue sky,
Where doves live and can be remembered,
Fallen, pure-blooded, loyal souls surrendered,
Where cupids, angels and gods from all religions
are members,
Where the good souls are defenders
And where mysterious beings, unidentified objects
and microscopic monsters live
And where the good clouds shine and the bad
clouds hide,
Where the mighty eagle flies with pride
And glides towards their prey at night,
Where the sky is calm as the shimmery, slick and
slender ocean waves out the sand.

Leah Bamotra (9)
Curwen Primary School, Plaistow

Hogwarts' Houses

Gryffindor awaits you
Do you have what it takes?
Your efforts are due,
There is no room for mistakes,
Or maybe you're fit for Slytherin,
Where darkness awakes,
You can feel mischievousness simmering,
Your fate waits.
Ravenclaw anticipates for a wise and smart mind,
Those of wit,
Will always find their kind,
Perhaps you're set in Hufflepuff,
Where loyalty is key,
You might find it tough,
But nothing you can't achieve,
Now let the Sorting Hat do its magic
Trust me, it'll be fantastic!

Nushraalam Subha (10)
Curwen Primary School, Plaistow

Keep On Trying

Teamwork makes a dream work!
Resilience,
Everyone is unique but not everyone is Sikh,
Support others to make brothers,
Follow your dreams, I know it seems
Impossible!
But look at me, I know you can be
Anything
Remember you are unstoppable!
Remember you are unbeatable!
If you can believe you can achieve
Don't fear, resilience is here
Nothing can stop you from what you do
Keep trying and trying
Trying is the key if you can see
Nobody is perfect
Think positive
Stay positive.

Selena Hyder (8)
Curwen Primary School, Plaistow

Spring, Summer, Autumn And Winter

In a pretty little garden,
Flowers were blooming with joy
And out popped the little boys
Which meant spring was here.

Summer came
And painted everything green
Boys screamed
Splashing each other in a pool.

Autumn came and the leaves turned gold
And fell off the branches of the trees
Which made it look bold
The leaves crunch as you step on them.

Along came winter, freezing everything
And painting it all white
Barely anyone was outside
And the garden was out of life.

Claire Liu (7)
Curwen Primary School, Plaistow

The World Of Pollution

This is the world we live in
Like a bin that we walk within
We can do better!
The world is like a huge sweater
It hugs us tightly
So we should help it, even slightly

This is the word we spread:
It's this poem you should've read
Before our planet heats up
And turns infrared
But then all we could do was feel dread

These are the words I write:
Please save the planet
It's like a big, huge pomegranate
I beg you to help Earth
It's a test to prove your worth.

Courtney Wynter (11)
Curwen Primary School, Plaistow

The Beauty Of The World

The world is full of wonder and beauty all around,
From the mountains to the oceans, and the forests that abound.
The sun that shines so brightly, and the stars that twinkle at night,
The moon that casts its silver light and the birds that take flight.
The flowers that bloom in springtime and the leaves that fall in fall,
The snowflakes that dance in winter and the summer's beckoning call.
So take a moment to appreciate all the wonders of this place,
And let your heart be filled with joy as you gaze upon its face.

Bethel Adeniran (8)
Curwen Primary School, Plaistow

You Are Strong

When you are feeling sad
And starting to get mad
Just listen to my words
You are brave
You are strong
And you have been all along
Those who say you can't
Remove them from your mind
And don't let their words put you in a bind
You are brave
You are strong
And you have been all along
When you walk in a room
Walk with pride
And let confidence be your guide
Because you are brave
You are strong
And you have been all along.

Jasmine Peasah (8)
Curwen Primary School, Plaistow

Change Of Nature

My country is decorated by the beauty of nature,
We have lakes, mountains and beautiful creatures.
There are four seasons in my country,
Spring brings shine and glow.
Nature wakes up and plants grow.
Summer brings green leaves and sunlight.
Enjoy the night.
Autumn means red and gold is all around.
Leaves are falling on the ground.
Winter makes nature sleep.
Trees have no leaves.
When we say bye-bye to snow
Again flowers will grow.

Tahfeem Toshana (7)
Curwen Primary School, Plaistow

Football Dreams

In my dream
I was in a football team
Playing a game
But a player came
And tackled me
But hurt my knee
I went back
But I couldn't do that
I found it a bit hard
So the ref pulled a yellow card
I got the ball
And scored a goal
But my shirt
Got a bit of dirt
Ninety minutes ticking
While I'm still kicking
As long as I push up
I won't give up.

Humaira Harris (7)
Curwen Primary School, Plaistow

Harry Potter Houses

You might belong in Gryffindor
With the power of Dumbledore
They're daring and heroic

You might belong in Hufflepuff
Where they are loyal
Those patient Hufflepuffs are true

You might belong in Ravenclaw
Your mind will soar
With those of wit and learning

Or perhaps in Slytherin
You will make your real friends
These cunning folk use any means.

Raed Samee (10)
Curwen Primary School, Plaistow

Kindness, Kindness, Kindness

Kindness is the best way to go about life
Kindness is the way to strive
Don't pick and choose
Either way, you'll lose
Be kind every day
Be kind in every way
Be kind to each other
And everyone else you know
It's time to let your kindness show
Show kindness
Show it to everyone
'In a world where you can be anything
Be kind.'

Kristabel Kuagbela (8)
Curwen Primary School, Plaistow

Don't Give Up

If you keep on going and never stop
You can make it to the top
And keep on going
Life is full of struggles
Some are hard and some are easy
But if you don't give up
You will overcome them all
Try not to give up
And when you keep going
You make it work with everything you've got
Don't give up
And you will make it to the top.

Abiegail Jimenez (7)
Curwen Primary School, Plaistow

Silly Billy

S illy Billy, Silly Billy
I am Silly Billy
L ots of slime, Silly Billy
L oud music, Silly Billy
"Y ippee!" shouts Silly Billy

B read with jam, Silly Billy
I am Silly Billy
L ove gross Silly Billy
L etters dropping, Silly Billy
Y et it's time for bed, Silly Billy.

Huryra Chowdhury (9)
Curwen Primary School, Plaistow

My Friends

A friend is like a star that twinkles and glows,
Or maybe like an ocean that gently flows,
They hold you up when you are weak,
Helping you find what it is you seek,
A friend is like gold that you should treasure,
And take care of forever and ever,
Standing by all the way,
There to help you through your day,
A friend is more than one in a million.

Ibrahim Hussain (8)
Curwen Primary School, Plaistow

Amazing Cat

There was once a white cat
Who walked up and down the street
For he longed to meet a nice owner
With a nice and tasty treat

No owner appeared so instead
He sat on a mat
Eating a rat
In a really cold hat

The rat didn't make him feel better
So he went for a nap
He dreamed of a nice owner
In a warm and comfy house.

Amara Khan (8)
Curwen Primary School, Plaistow

Empathy

Never judge anyone by their looks,
About their life or what they do,
You could never know what someone else is going through,
Kindness doesn't cost anything,
Try to be as kind as an angel,
Treat others how you want to be treated,
Never be rude,
Because you haven't walked in... their shoes,
Show empathy, it's what we should choose!

Anushka Dhir (10)
Curwen Primary School, Plaistow

Unicorns In The Sky

U nicorns have long, sparkly horns
N ever say unicorns are bad or not real
I actually believe in unicorns
C ute, cuddly baby unicorns can be your pet
O ver the sea, under the sky, the unicorn will fly
R est with unicorns in your heart
N ice days with unicorns start!

Clarissa Jones (8)
Curwen Primary School, Plaistow

Young Soldier Boy

Young soldier boy walked through a road,
Young soldier boy held death in his hands...
Young soldier boy held it with all his might,
Young soldier boy fought hard and tough,
Young soldier boy saw war and death,
Then he walked down the path off a cliff.
Crash! He went down and never came back...

Laila Bouchaib (10)
Curwen Primary School, Plaistow

Hopes And Dreams

I look upon the starry night
And all my troubles seem to fly,
In hopes that dreams will come my way
And I have faith in my new day,
I don't need to worry about a thing
Because my heart will jump and sing.
My hopes will rise into the sky
And with its might, it'll fly high.

Brey Rimando (8)
Curwen Primary School, Plaistow

My Family Dog

Black nose
White socks
Fur fading from rust to bright white

Always playing
Having fun
She's a puppy-shaped jack-in-a-box

Sleeping fluffball
Seeking love
The first face I see when I come down in the
morning is...

My dog, Scout!

Benji Nicholls (8)
Curwen Primary School, Plaistow

Queen Of Nice

If you feel happy or sad, angry or bad,
I'll be there for you.
Friends have to care and share
And be a ray of sunshine on a cloudy day and play.
I was talking to a llama and it gave me this advice:
"You've got to be the queen of nice."

Khaleesi Jones-Desilva (8)
Curwen Primary School, Plaistow

What Are Dreams?

D reams are your imagination,
R oaming in your mind,
E very time you sleep you dream,
A lthough they're sometimes bad or kind,
M ost people forget the dreams they've seen. We all have dreams.

Danica Yesan (9)
Curwen Primary School, Plaistow

Down Days

If you are down,
Or you're feeling blue,
Or maybe a frown,
I know what to do.

Pick yourself up,
Have a little cry,
Maybe drink a 7 Up,
Don't be shy,
Tell someone!

Diego Bernardino Alves Dos Santos (10)
Curwen Primary School, Plaistow

Spring

S pring birds sing
P lants grow
R ainbows show
I nsects come out
N ice weather starts to come
G reen grass starts to grow.

Ismail Miah (7)

Curwen Primary School, Plaistow

Mother Nature

I am watching trees be cut down,
My creations are getting sad;
Animals are going to drown.
Oh help me, oh help me, oh help me!

Whatever can I do?
Soon I'll be destroyed,
This is because of you;
I'm hopeless, I'm hopeless, I'm hopeless.

What can you see?
I see a world of cruel,
Look what you're doing to me;
Oh save me, oh save me, oh save me!

First it was one animal,
Now it's a whole jungle;
I want something to happen that's magical.
I'm dying, I'm dying, I'm dying!

Georgia Palin (9)
Farington Primary School, Farington

I Am The Fire

I am the fire,
I am nature's slayer.
I am the monster of the forest.
Humans say I'm the meanest.

I take down everything in my way.
But if it's water, it beats me at my own game
I've burned down many animals' homes.
You can call me griefsome.

When I burn anything, I always leave a trace,
At least I burned trees because I'm so ace.
Or maybe some bird eggs on the floor.
Or maybe the whole thing in ashes, I've done
it before.

Sometimes people summon me to burn all
the heather,
Others summon me to delete their structure,
But most important is the rainforests.
I'm a huge terrorist to florists.

I am the fire,
I am nature's slayer,
I am the monster of the forest.
Nature says I'm the meanest.

Zahra Randall (10)
Farington Primary School, Farington

Amazon Rainforest

I walk back home,
To see lots of destruction.
Animals all dead,
Humans making new construction.

Trees gone,
All this deforestation.
It needs to stop,
It's making a big situation.

Animals not breathing,
Including our organisation.
Humans are bad,
We need some medication.

All their weapons,
And determination,
Is way too high
And leading to our annihilation.

Animals taken away,
For lots of testing.

All forced to go,
Without any resting.

Riley Unitt (10)
Farington Primary School, Farington

My Journey To End

I watched the sunset,
The horizon it met.
The tall trees blew,
Not for long because of you.

You destroyed my home,
Now I'm all alone.
I will use all my determination,
Because of this horrible deforestation.

I'm running out of time,
Because of this crime.
I went on my way
To find where I shall lay.

I watched the sunset,
For death I met.
The tall trees blew,
For I died because of you.

Please stop
You've damaged a lot.

Lucy Broadhurst (9)
Farington Primary School, Farington

Rainforest

See the dolphins swimming away,
The little jaguars happy as they play,
The baby birds flying above,
The stingray stinging.

Wildlife are hunting,
Leaping and annoying,
The space they just passed.

The waterfall is dripping,
Water is sparkling,
Fish are swimming in deep water.

So I know they're half a world away,
Rainforest I can't see,
But I can learn and understand,
Because the future starts with me.

Darcie Bilsborough (9)
Farington Primary School, Farington

Orange Orangutan

Orange orangutan,
Swinging in the trees.
Hi, hello,
It's me!

Living in the jungle,
It is my biome.
Until these nasty people,
Destroy my home.

The trees are destroyed,
To build an organisation.
Who can help me,
In this bad situation?

Less of me,
By the day.
I pray these stupid people,
Would go away.

This madness must end,
I'm leaving it with you.

Please help me,
This can't continue.

Sonny Benson (10)
Farington Primary School, Farington

I'm A Sloth

I'm a sloth, sitting in a tree,
Chilling, being as cute as can be.
Hey! Hello!
It's me!

I'm really hoping you see me,
Instead of cutting down my tree!
Are you sure this is the way?
Me nor my tree are your prey!

I hate all this deforestation,
You've left me without family, in isolation!
When will you realise?
You are killing my friends, oh my eyes!

So stop deforestation!

Nathan Morement (10)
Farington Primary School, Farington

Mother Nature

M y Earth

O ur Earth

T ogether you're destroying it

H ere you live, there is no

E arth number two, the only one you're on

R ight now is the only

N ow is your only chance

A nd before my last words

T reat the Earth kindly

U nless you want to be extinct

R un while you can

E xtinction is coming soon.

Lola Masterman (10)
Farington Primary School, Farington

Wild Nature

Worries taking over
A bite causing a blood overflow
Running through the fathomless forest
Wet sweat burst out

Animals dribble
From the trees of victims
Screaming please, please, please

Water gushing down the trees
Wherever you go water is in sight and seen

Out in the wilderness
Killers lurk in the trees that should be seen.

Jake Harbour (9)
Farington Primary School, Farington

Amazon Rainforest

All the animals running,
Far far away.
All the predators chomping,
Even today.

All the animals running,
Far far away.
All the poachers hunting,
Right now today.

We can't stop today,
No matter how hard we try,
So try and help out,
And soon it might be solved.

Michael Haynes (10)
Farington Primary School, Farington

Climate Change

Climate change occurs
People don't care
Adults cut down trees
They aren't fair

Death is near
Fear is here
Our final breath is near
So our goodbyes are here

Look at the sky
Look at the ground
As the sky is polluted
The ground is littered.

Nadia Struska (10)
Farington Primary School, Farington

Siblings

S iblings, siblings
I love my siblings
B rothers and sisters, always taking care
L ove your siblings
I love my brother because he is my sibling
N ever hate your siblings even if they hurt you
G ive your love to your siblings and they will give
    love back
S iblings are the best!

Pantelina Cappalonga (9)
Ponsbourne St Mary's CE Primary School, Hertford

Birdie Flew Away

Birdie and I,
We play together,
We eat together,
We work together at school,
We sit together,
We laugh together,
We are kind with each other,
We help each other,
One day, Birdie flew away.
Really far away.
I miss my Birdie.
I hope one day I can fly to see her again.

Marina Louca (8)
Ponsbourne St Mary's CE Primary School, Hertford

Brothers

B rothers are for life
R ays of sunshine
O ak is my favourite tree
T oys are the best
H arry is my best friend
E pic friendship lasts forever
R eally work together
S paghetti is the best dinner.

Anthony Jordan (9)
Ponsbourne St Mary's CE Primary School, Hertford

Burrito

B urritos are the best
U se peppers and vegetables, it's my favourite
R ubbish is not a word in Mexican food
R adish is nice in burritos
I love them
T omato sauce is nice
O nly I like veggie burritos.

Berri-Rae Pryor (9)
Ponsbourne St Mary's CE Primary School, Hertford

Rocco Pup

R occo is respectful
O range balls everywhere
C anine cutey
C ute paws
O h how lovely Rocco is

P erfectly huggable puppy
U nbelievable fur
P iece of cake.

Anastasia Tsekouras (8)
Ponsbourne St Mary's CE Primary School, Hertford

Love

L ife is hard but the people you love help you
O ne of the greatest things is to forgive
V ery simply, the ones you love will always be there
E veryone, look how far we've come on the journey of life.

Gabriella Delfino (7)

Ponsbourne St Mary's CE Primary School, Hertford

Cars

The wonderful hobby of cars!
The McLarens, so beautiful
Lamborghinis, best cars ever
Bugattis, super fast
Tesla, overrated
Ferrari, 2nd best car ever
Koenigsegg, really fast cars!

Alexander Papaleontiou (8)
Ponsbourne St Mary's CE Primary School, Hertford

If I Were...

If I were a rabbit I would want to be a flower
If I were a flower I would want to be a bee
If I were a bee I would want to be a guinea pig
If I were a guinea pig I would want to be an
elephant.

Naomi Lilley (7)
Ponsbourne St Mary's CE Primary School, Hertford

My Music

M usic is special, music is fun
U se it together with everyone
S ing up high or sing down low
I love my music wherever it may go
C an you hear the music?

Evie Spafford (9)
Ponsbourne St Mary's CE Primary School, Hertford

What Do You See In The Future Ahead?

Today, a girl came over and talked to me,
She said, "Ahead of you, what do you see?"
I gazed around like a clueless sheep,
And peered around her to have a peep.
I responded, "Litter by a birch tree."

She shook her head and pointed past my ears,
"What would you like to see in a couple of years?"
I itched my head and thought with all my mind,
"A world without war and violence of some kind.
A place without hunger, issues or tears!"

Then she displayed a gleaming, clean grin,
"What about climate change and how our planet
has been?"
I answered with a quote from a person I knew:
'There are no passengers on spaceship Earth; we
are all the crew'.
A statement I agree with and would draw people
in.

In the blink of an eye, the girl had gone,
I looked around and began to yawn,
Was it all just a mysterious dream?
Maybe a youthful prankster's scheme?
But still, I believe happiness is the route to follow
on!

Maia Cooper (11)
Send CE Primary School, Send

Moon Animals

The moon tiger is a tiger that has two colours,
purple and blue
The stripes are a galaxy blue and the rest is purple.

The moon cat is a small but long cat
And you can't see it at night
The tail is white and the feet are purple
And the rest is blue.

The moon dog is a bit like a Golden Retriever
In the day it is the normal colour (white)
But at night it turns blue on the body and head
But purple on the tail, legs and feet
But they are very skinny.

The moon rabbit is a galaxy rabbit that is white
like the moon
And the tail is purple and it has blue, sparkling
eyes
It only comes out at night so you can't see it.

The moon hedgehog is a galaxy, spiky circle that is
three times the size

The peach is blue while the spikes are white and purple with stars
It hides underground in the day and comes out at night.

Kai Cooper (9)
Send CE Primary School, Send

A Recipe For A Good Friend

If you mix and blend a very good friend,
You will need these values to succeed.
The values that make a good friend are,
Kindness, patience, love and fun.
If you mix these together you will find
That you have one very good friend.
Sprinkle on trust then mix in some happiness too,
And never forget that they will always love you.
No matter what happens, they will be there for
you.
Sharing is caring, that's what friends do,
Look out for each other and your friendship is true.
Don't leave them out whenever you play
And always make sure that they have a very good
day.
Help them up when they fall down
And turn their frown upside down.
Show them you care, always be there
And never forget that this friend could be the best
one yet.

Betsy Anscombe (8)
Send CE Primary School, Send

The Dream Of A Young Footballer

Underneath the boundless sky, so high,
A ten-year-old boy, with a twinkle in his eye.
Learning English words in a playful chase,
Dreaming of football in a vast open space.
"Hello" "Goodbye" "Goal" and "Pass"
A year of words flowing smooth as glass.
Ten short years and dreams taken flight,
On the football pitch, under the stadium lights.
Through tales of games, his passion unfurls,
His dreams as round as the football whirls.
In every word, every kick, every roll,
Football and language stirring his soul.
A boy of ten, in life's grand play,
With football dreams, he'll find his way.
May the world cheer for his brave endeavour,
In football and learning, dreams last forever.

Azaan Afsar (10)
Send CE Primary School, Send

When I Saw A Dinosaur

The day I saw a dinosaur it had a big round belly.
When I saw a dinosaur it had a big round belly and
sharp claws.
When I saw a dinosaur it had a big round belly,
sharp claws and big red eyes.
When I saw a dinosaur it had a big belly, sharp
claws, big red eyes and pink, sparkly skin.
When I saw a dinosaur it had a big round belly,
sharp claws, big red eyes, pink, sparkly skin and big
feet.
The day I saw a dinosaur it had a big round belly,
sharp claws, big red eyes, pink, sparkly skin, big
feet and fluffy yellow fur patches.
When I saw a dinosaur it had a big round belly,
sharp claws, big red eyes, pink, sparkly skin, big
feet and fluffy yellow fur patches but staring at the
dinosaur for so long got me tired of the view
Now I am sharing it with you.

Betsy Stevens (10)
Send CE Primary School, Send

Values

Love is a value we show every day,
Respect is a value you show in your way.
Responsibility is when you're on your own,
But friendship will never let you alone.

Character is when you show your true self,
Like cleaners or builders or even an elf.
Self-control is when you control your feelings,
So you don't fly up with large, heavy wings.

Values are wise and always mature,
But when you show values don't ask for more.
Because sometimes when you're a bit impolite,
You won't show a value at all in that night.

Values are good, values are pure,
And they definitely help you, that I am sure.

Eyleen Marcel (10)
Send CE Primary School, Send

Animals Of The Rainforest

Bulbous-billed toucan squawking in the sunlight,
Cool, pristine feathers, trapezing through the trees.

Segmented serpent, grappling at dinner time,
Tightening and crushing, struggling to squeeze.

Flame-pelted orang swinging through the canopy,
Feasting on fruitlets in the dappled light.

Jet-black jaguar, murky as obsidian,
Sulking in the shadows, silent in the night.

We need to care about conservation, we need to
stop deforestation,
These awful actions of mankind mean animals will
be hard to find,
If we take the time to care, these wild creatures
will be less rare.

Helena Collins (8)
Send CE Primary School, Send

Harry Potter's Friends

Here is a challenge for you to solve, about Harry's friends young and old...

Riddle 1
He is resilient and strong
He won a fight against his enemy
From Dumbledore he got a deluminator
He was a keeper in Quidditch.

Riddle 2
She is kind and caring
She is the smartest in her year
From Dumbledore she got a book
She had a time turner.

Riddle 3
He is brave and tall
He delivered Hedwig in Diagon Alley
Dumbledore gave him trust and let him teach
He loves unusual creatures.

Answers: 1. Ron. 2. Hermione. 3. Hagrid.

Florence Booth (9)
Send CE Primary School, Send

My Best Friend And I

My best friend and I have so much fun
Our favourite thing to do is play out in the sun

We look up high into the sky above
And know that we are always surrounded by love

We both have a very annoying brother
I hope my mum and dad don't have another!

The best thing about you being my friend
Is to know you will be there until the very end

Being a good friend is learning to care
But also not forgetting to learn how to share

We've come to the end of my poem, you see,
We must hurry up or we'll be late for our tea!

Eliza Attwater (8)
Send CE Primary School, Send

Wonders Of Nature

The sky is as blue as the sea,
The grass is glossy and green,
The children run around playing, dancing,
Singing, humming, all day long.

The swaying trees with the blustering wind, twirling
around like a ballerina,
The hot, blistering sun shines through the treetops.

We can help. We can save.
The environment is our home.
All the plastic is not okay.
We all have a role to play.
If everybody helps,
The wildlife will be safe.

The amazing trees, animals and wildlife should
always be taken of.

Ava-Rose Downey (10)
Send CE Primary School, Send

Betty The Norfolk Terrier

Betty is my dog
My sweet little dog.
She has been in my life
For as long as I remember.
She came to our family
Thirteen years ago
To fill with love all our life.
She is cheeky and bright,
And a piggy sometimes.
She likes food of all kinds but
Her favourite is bacon rind.
We take her for long walks around the lake,
But she really prefers to swim like a hake.
She is my big sister and I love her a lot.
The best dog in the world, thanks a lot.

Tomasina Gallagher (9)
Send CE Primary School, Send

River Place

I sit in class sad and alone
In my own zone
Waiting for class to be done!
I slip on my shoes
And run right ahead to my mom.
I get back home and have a snack
Then go back!
I walk out the gate
With no one around,
No sound in the distance,
No ducks to be seen.
I pull out my book
And dip my toes in.
I look in there
And everything moves.
I look in the water
And I can see you
Right on the riverside
On the river place.

Megan Biddles (8)
Send CE Primary School, Send

English Bull Terriers And Their Life

When you have an English Bull Terrier there is a lot to know
So here is something that tells you so.
They are the most loyal and loving dogs you will ever meet
And they will never accept defeat.
They are also fun and make me laugh when they lick my feet,
Although they are cheeky and sweet.

They give you courage and bravery, you see,
That's all a part of having a little bully,
With their heart, they will care
And that is why I wrote this song.

Indira Wilkinson (9)
Send CE Primary School, Send

Holidays

On holiday I might go to the beach,
Or go to the shop, one pound each.
Then I'll have fun at the shore,
Or watch Descendants (rotten to the core).
After that, I'll climb a tree,
Or shall I count from one to three?
Twirling in the pretty sun,
It will be so much fun.
Make a crumble,
To make my tummy rumble.
Mermaids splash along the sea,
While the goblins drink their tea.
It's nearly the end of May,
Time to go on holiday.

Chlea Marcel (7)
Send CE Primary School, Send

My Cat, Poppy

I love my cat,
She is thin but not fat.
She sleeps on my bed,
And licks my head.
She is black and white,
And very light.
She leaps and bounds,
Across the ground.
She poses near the roses.
She sniffs and smells,
All the bluebells.
She catches the mice,
Not once but twice.
Her ears flick,
When she hears the birds click.
A dog walks by, sees Poppy and barks,
Poppy runs and farts!

Lucy Middleton (7)
Send CE Primary School, Send

The Wonky And A Smile Were Racing

I'm sorry, my teacher, for being so late,
Well, I was with my mate,
And we were walking to school,
When I started to drool.

'Cause I saw a crocodile,
It had a big smile,
It was dancing with a bug
Who looked very smug.

They were with something wonky,
It seemed to be a donkey,
Well, we rode them on the racing course,
Well you see, Miss Kate,
That's why I'm late.

Scout Marshall (10)
Send CE Primary School, Send

A Lost Journey

Along the mountains, across the sea
Lies beneath is a coral reef, inside is every fish
Black, blue, colours galore, all you can dream of
and more
Then I move on and on
Just to find a beach
On the beach I stay for days and days, finding fish
to eat
Until one day a ship comes by
I wave until my arm falls off
Then all I can hear with my old brittle ears
All I can hear is...
Bye.

Eve Ellis (9)
Send CE Primary School, Send

Mystic Wolves Of Midnight Valley

If you run with me I am eternity
In and out of a woodland forest
Birds sing a friendly chorus
My coat glimmers in the midnight light
Howling at the moon
Daylight is coming soon!
The leaves connect to all the trees
The wolves like me all run free
The clouds glow in a luminous way
Guiding the owls out of the day
If you step foot in any den
It'll be an early end!

Madison Poley (10)
Send CE Primary School, Send

My Golf Day

Whilst I get my golf club out,
I need some trainers to walk about,
Then I get in the car,
I need a ball to hit far,
Then I take a shot,
But I find myself tied up in a knot,
So I try another swing,
To become the pin-seeking king,
Satisfied with what I've hit,
I then go home for a long sit,
Another day has gone past,
I hope tomorrow will be a blast.

Amelie Rogers (9)
Send CE Primary School, Send

Alfie, My Precious Cat

I love Alfie, he is my cat,
After school, he waits for me on my doormat,
If he's not there he'll be on my bed,
Ready for bedtime and a stroke of his head,
He gets me gifts of birds and mice,
I'd much rather have a cake or cream slice,
But that's his way of showing he loves me,
So I will never be angry as I am his mummy,
I love Alfie.

Poppy Banks (7)
Send CE Primary School, Send

Send School

S end C of E
E ngaging with PE
N othing is too hard
D etermined to keep on trying

S end C of E
C lass teachers are cool
H elping children
O f this school
O ccupies us
L oving the school!

Jessica Woods (8)
Send CE Primary School, Send

Summer Fun

I love summer, it's so fun!
We get to play all day
We paddle on the water's edge
Down in Swanage Bay
We eat ice cream in the sun
And in the arcade, I like to play
We watch Swanage Carnival (that's a big parade)
And everything I see makes me shout yay!

Mia Drummond (8)
Send CE Primary School, Send

A Great Adventure

Climb to the heights of the towering mountains,
Plunge into the azure depths of the sea,
A long-lost city of dreams lies within,
To discover a place of belonging, a solace unseen,
Enrich yourself in its glistening treasure,
Building your strength and bearing its power.

Mali Reuben (8)
Send CE Primary School, Send

Dogs

I have a dog called Pippa
And she loves to chew my slipper.
My friend has a dog, Maisy,
Which is very fat and lazy.
They play in the park
So they can bark.
On the other hand, my child has a dog called Spot
And he is covered in snot!
Spot likes music!

Sienna Stafford (7)
Send CE Primary School, Send

Breaking Through The Finish Line

R apid wind blowing against me

U sing my arms to push me forward

N ot giving up

N ot me, not now!

I am breaking out

N ot stopping until victory is mine

G lory as I bolt through the finish line.

Ada Reuben (8)
Send CE Primary School, Send

The Door

A ringing or a knocking
Either one works
A noise from the door
The clock ticks in time for the door
Animals wait by the door
Waiting for the moment
The door opens.

Flora Bricklebank (10)
Send CE Primary School, Send

I Love Dogs

My dog likes tickles
He also likes to wiggle
He is big
And he likes to dig
And he eats like a pig
He likes to rip paper
He never awakens
He eats bacon.

Jessica Simmons (7)
Send CE Primary School, Send

Sloths

The slow sloth starts his day
Eating leaves on his way
Sluggishly moving, no time to play
The smiling sloth sleeps today
Sleep, sleep,
Sleep,
Sleep.

Emily Harrison (9)
Send CE Primary School, Send

Harry The Epic Wizard

There once was a wizard called Harry
A witch he desired to marry
He knew a lot of spells
Was filled with magic cells
But broomsticks are heavy to carry.

Ben Warne (9)
Send CE Primary School, Send

The Woods

I crept cautiously through the damp, windy woods,
As I saw the dead end sign,
I started to freak out while the silence stretched
out from the long branches,
I began to walk on further like a fierce bat,
I stopped to see a small old cottage,
The trees started to whisper,
I stepped inside and sat down on the creaky
wooden chair,
While heavy breathing filled the air.

A while after, I lit the candles near the fireplace,
I heard a knock on the door and went to open it,
Until I saw nobody was there,
Bang! My blood ran cold.

The Northern Lights were now turned off,
As I heard a scratch from a dangerous cat,
The wind had stopped and some light,
I stepped outside to look at the creepy sight.

Jessica O'Reilly (10)
St Matthew's Primary School, Luton

The Secret Lair

As it got gloomy through the day
I scouted the forest night and day.
As I explored I heard a door. *Bang.*
My heart told me to run but my brain told me to get closer
But instead, I went to the campsite.

Walking alone and palms bone dry,
I got a strange feeling that there was someone behind,
I started to run faster and faster,
While out of breath
I was getting closer.

Should I risk my life by stopping and taking a breath
Or keep pushing?
Once I made it to the campsite I looked in the tents
No one was there.
I started to panic.

I calmed myself down and went in my tent.
When I almost went to sleep I saw a secret lair...

The sound of footsteps were nearing closer,
As quick as a flash I started to run,
Souls taking my breath bit by bit,
The roots were like a trap waiting for me to trip.

Gaining the courage to turn around I did,
But the only thing I saw was a derelict horizon with
some mist,
A whisper caught my attention,
It said, "You can't see me but I can see you"
As a bony hand grabbed my shoulder and pulled
me away,
Now I can only wait and accept my fate.

Now I haunt the ones that dare to do the forest
quest.

Kuba Dąbrowski (11)
St Matthew's Primary School, Luton

Place Of Unknown

Dark, deadly, deserted, a place where screams
sound
Like deafening spells.
Dead leaves dancing with the rusty air but
The place is not fair!
The lifeless place is no more alive but the alive
ones are the fake ones.
The air is heavier than tones.

Drip, drip, drip, the rain never stops.
Up, up, up, the top is the wiggly tops.
The place is not fair!

When you hit the hay, the voices are the annoying
spells.
The dark is the definition of the spirits of hells.
The awfully good smells were the sweet rain,
When it hits your skin, it's only pain.
There's no sunshine, it's only the dark moonshine,
But it never shines,
It will ever shine when the owl fades
And the falling rain turns into tiers of clouds.

The place is not fair.
Never speak or the word of your own will vanish you.
Tie your mouth or you're going to die here!
There's only one thing you'll have to worry about,
The blood-curdling, headless creature,
It will only chase if you say the name thrice.
The only things alive are you and your dog, Dice,
Good luck in your next dreams - the place...

Huzaifa Malik (11)
St Matthew's Primary School, Luton

The Abandoned House

As I walked through the...
Forest, I suddenly got lost.
As I saw skeleton bones everywhere
I felt terrified.
As I took a step I saw a huge abandoned house.

As I approached the door
My heart was beating as fast as lightning.
As I heard a crack
I knew it was something behind me.
As I looked back
There was nothing behind me.
When I entered the abandoned house
It was dark and silent.

I tried to not make noises
But I was hearing silent screaming.

Drip, drip, drip, my mouth went dry.
It was an exhausting moment but I couldn't
give up.
Quick as a flash, something surrounded me!

Traumatisingly, I didn't know what to do.

After a couple of minutes,
The spirits were gone.
I was trying to run away
But I knew something was gonna stop me.
So I did a loud bang in a different room so I could escape.

After I escaped I tried to find a way to get out of the forest.
I took each step at a time,
I looked everywhere.
I found the exit but it was surrounded by lots of trees.
As I took steps to it
I heard whispering echoes...

Ioana Supuran (11)
St Matthew's Primary School, Luton

The Unknown Graveyard

One night I heard a knock
I looked at the night sky
Knock, knock, knock
My house was ice-cold
Drip, drip, drip, the ceiling began to leak
I took one step at a time

I took one step at a time
My massive, heavy wooden door creaked open
All there was was complete silence
Then I heard a bass drum of a knock
I heard loud footsteps
I was all alone

Someone was approaching my front door
I heard my creaky floorboard creak
I was so flustered
I thought there was a killer
I had to write in my journal

That one night I was so flustered
I knew someone was behind me

I went to the graveyard
The graveyard door slammed shut
The door was jammed
I fell and looked back
It was pitch-black

I was so flustered that the streetlight went out
Then someone came into the cemetery
The spooky spirits had pinned me down to the
ground as I tried getting up
It was a relief after
I got up and ran
That was just like a nightmare
But something on my body was gushing out
with blood
It was my stomach.

Tallulah Kingham (11)
St Matthew's Primary School, Luton

The Frightening Killer

In my haunted house,
I was resting in my enormous bed,
Chilling like a koala,
Was playing on my plain phone,
Deafening silence filled the air,

Drip, drip, drip, the rain continuously fell,
Knock, knock, there was a noise,
I was panicking and flustered,
I had to go check,
I had to see what was there,

I was strolling slowly like a sloth, looking around,
My heart was drumming, fast,
Knock, knock, I heard it again,
Just then, the door slowly opened and whilst
greeting me
I became more cautious,

I approached the dusty door,
Then a dark, shadowy figure popped out,
As it got nearby, stood a vicious killer,

Its garments red as blood,
And his silver, shiny knife pointing at me,
threatening death,

It was the most sinister assassin I had ever seen!
With fear, I ran rapidly away from the killer,
But not too long, the killer was lightning,
It caught me, took his knife and *slash!*
Oops, he got me.

Roland Takacs (11)
St Matthew's Primary School, Luton

The Ghost Children

The ghost child,
No one wild, spicy or mild.
They are see-through,
And will always watch your every move.

Although you can't see them,
Whish, whoosh, they go through your empty hallways.
Their powerful pressure, one as cold as ice,
A pressure giving you the coldest shiver down your spine.

They can hear you although you can't hear them.
They can chase you although you can't chase them.
They can even possess you although you can't.

They once dreamt of tying the knot before they
Disastrously died.
They're not one but four;
Two ghost girls and two ghost boys.
And are looking forward to eating those
Delicious yet dancing organs of yours...

Up till now, they're still around,
Not making a single sound.
Don't be startled when you get to know,
They are watching you nice and slow.
Who am I kidding? You will meet them soon.
Who knows? They might even be sitting right next to you.

Ginelle Ofosu-Appiah (11)
St Matthew's Primary School, Luton

Alone

Alone in the derelict, decrepit house,
The deafening silence pinned me to the ground,
Tap, tap, tap, fear filled the room,
The night sky lit up by the sweating moon.

Alone in the derelict, decrepit house,
My heart a beating drum,
That's when I found,
A bony hand lying there making me feel numb.

Alone in the derelict, decrepit house,
Silent screams filled the air,
Like an enormous crowd,
In the mist I saw a dark shadow tugging on a girl's hair,
I stood there paralysed trying not to make a sound.

Alone in the derelict, decrepit house,
The deadly demon looked me up and down,
It tied me up in knots and devoured my fingers,
Blood spewed out, the death signs lingered.

Alone in the derelict, decrepit house,
My life was like a roller coaster,
My emotions flying around,
Who knew if the notorious beast has been found,
Now that I've hit the headstones.

Tia-Marie Stewart (11)
St Matthew's Primary School, Luton

At Midnight, All Alone

They will notice you whatever you do,
Although you can't see them, they can see you.

Knock, knock, knock, I open the door widely ajar,
But there is no figure there or afar.
They will notice you whatever you do,
Although you can't see them, they can see you.

I creep down the road to locate the stalker,
But despite my search, I am the only walker.
They will notice you whatever you do,
Although you can't see them, they can see you.

I walk to the graveyard beneath the night sky, my
mouth suddenly goes dry,
The deafening silence makes me cry.
They will notice you whatever you do,
Although you can't see them, they can see you.

The clock strikes midnight and I know it's time for
me to go.
My fate is sealed, I guess so.

They will notice you whatever you do,
They can see you; now, you can see them too...

Zuzanna Manuszewska (10)
St Matthew's Primary School, Luton

Alone In The Mystifying Forest

As the eerie silence swallowed me whole,
A loud bang pierced my ear,
Running forward, tall, towering trees endlessly
going on,
And clusters of leaves tripping me over.

A pack of wolves howling at the night sky,
A sudden shiver ran down my spine,
One step after the other, *crack!*
Someone was watching me.

My heart started beating like a drum,
Seconds went by, my fingers suddenly went numb,
The sound of breathing filled the air,
As quick as a flash, a pitch-black figure ran by.

As I rushed down the lane of everlasting trees,
Drip, drip, drip! A mysterious noise caught my ear,
I needed to find a way out of this strange forest,
My body was trembling with fear.

There was no way out,
The forest was not letting me go,

I wanted to scream,
Until a hidden creature snatched me.

Sunaina Ayesha (11)
St Matthew's Primary School, Luton

The Dark Forest

One night I was chilling at the forest,
It was dark, I did start to walk,
Then I started to hear noises,
I felt like someone was staring,
It felt ice-cold.

I went down to this tree,
Then I felt someone pulling me down,
I screamed, I started running,
But it felt like I was going around.

Drip, drip, drip, it started raining,
I was shivering then bright lightning,
I screamed, I saw the tree smiling at me.

I saw a dark shadow, I screamed,
I fell to the floor.
When I woke up I still did not know what
happened,
But when I saw the blood I did understand.
I was a ghost.

There was a policeman.
I wanted to tell him but he couldn't hear me.
He couldn't see me.
I cried.
He couldn't hear me.

I want to get revenge.
I can't because I am a ghost.

Fjorela Kasa (10)
St Matthew's Primary School, Luton

The Room

You wake in a waiting room,
It looks just like the old and abandoned one at the hospital.
You also see a muddly brown-coloured wooden door.
You have decided to walk towards it.

Step, step, step...
You open the door, tempted.
To your surprise, it's the same room...
But something is different,
It must be.

The silence stretches around the room,
You start noticing the difference...
It's the size! You finally notice!

But wait...
The same muddy brown-coloured and tempting door is there too,
You decide to continue opening the weird yet mysterious doors,
The size only gets smaller and smaller like mixed clothes in a washing machine.

Each time you open the doors you only get tempted more and more.

That's when you notice it's still the same exact room.

Zuzanna Janko (10)
St Matthew's Primary School, Luton

The One That Lurks

It hunts terrifyingly in dark places
Like a predator who hasn't eaten for days
It lurks in the silence of night
Slaughtering those in its petrifying presence

Heart racing, nowhere to run
Nowhere to hide, just stand still
Be ready to meet a horrifying demise

It moves soundlessly and deceitfully
It may have a toothless grin but you shall see its
razor-sharp teeth
It is as tall as a mountain but you can't see it

When you sense it, don't look, it will make you do
horrible things
It has a dreadful aroma of rotten flesh
It devours your lifeless soul
The ground cries as your body hits the ground

Its body covers you like a dark blanket
You feel your energy leaving your body

You feel ice-cold
You feel like you're dying.

Ameer Ali (11)
St Matthew's Primary School, Luton

Ella

Children are fair,
Children are young,
But despite what is heard,
What you hear from the tongue,

For down the staircase,
And beyond the walls,
Through the wretched tunnel,
A young girl calls,

Upon a velvet seat,
A dishevelled room,
In the blinding dark,
In the eerie gloom,

Take great caution,
You may be to blame,
You may lose your life,
You may lose your brain,

Wind calling desperately,
The walls cry warning,

Ella is born at night,
And dies at morning,

At the snap of a finger,
At the drop of a hat,
Many fall into her
So twisted trap,

For centuries upon centuries,
Victims are snatched like mice,
Venture out too far,
And pay the price.

Ismail Hogan (11)
St Matthew's Primary School, Luton

Hide-And-Seek

It's my turn to seek,
But it would be cheating to peek.
I shut my eyes,
Count to twenty-five,
Where are they going to hide?

Ready or not, here I come.
Give me a clue or even some.
As the wind howls,
And hoots come from owls,
I walk around like a lost puppy.
Where have they hidden?

"Ring around the Rosie, a pocket full of posies."
That must be my clue.
I walk through the graveyard to see who.
But it isn't someone I recognise,
She has a knife and blood-red eyes.
Where should I hide?

I run and I run,
This is not what I call having fun.

She is a monster,
Full of bloodthirst.
She isn't seeking.
But she finds me first.
Where should I have hidden?

Taylor Gardner (11)
St Matthew's Primary School, Luton

The Night's Embrace

In the old, abandoned house,
Where the walls are full of louse.
Ghosts come out to roam,
And make the place their home.

They rattle chains and moan,
Their presence felt but never shown.
Their stories lost to ongoing time,
Their souls forever intertwined.

So if you hear a whisper or a sigh,
Or see a figure passing by,
Remember that ghosts are nigh,
And they'll never say goodbye.

They haunt the long halls and wide rooms,
Their spirits trapped in endless glooms.
Their voices like tortured souls,
Their eyes like smouldering coals.

The shadows are living things,
Creeping up on you with wings.

The silence is a suffocating weight,
A reminder of your inevitable fate.

Witek Pelka (10)
St Matthew's Primary School, Luton

The Hunt

Every step I take I break a rule,
My heart is racing like never before,
As I look around *boom!* Something
Drops like a statue, I see the chair
And get a scare.

I walk and walk and stop in my tracks,
What I see is not to be told,
I continue to walk but what is that
Sound? I am then pinned by silence.

I go to sit but not on air,
I look for the chair but it is not there,
Did it run or hide away?
I fall asleep just before midnight.

I hear *drip, drip, drip* on the ceiling,
I take a peek for what I can seek,
But nothing there, I go back to bed,
Just after one more peep.

I get away to stay alive,
And here I am, I got away
To be here today.

Tyrese Turner (11)
St Matthew's Primary School, Luton

Death Envelops Me

Dormant souls lie within the forest
Terrified twigs snap between my feet
The deafening thunder roars like an angry lion
Echoing wails and screams pierce the silent night

Dormant souls lie within the forest
Their whispers and blood-curdling screams echo
throughout
The icy hot wind howls around me
Towering trees standing together like an army

Dormant souls lie within the forest
Shadows lurking behind the trees
They mark my footsteps as they closely approach
me
Shadows creep up behind me, ready to trap me in
eternal darkness

Dormant souls lie within the forest
I hope for the best for I don't know what's next
As I become enveloped in darkness, never to be
seen again...

Ethan Mlambo (11)
St Matthew's Primary School, Luton

The House Of Hell

The walls have ears and mirrors have eyes,
He's watching me, waiting to see me die.
I can hear screams and deadly shouts,
Blood dripping, it's all a plan.
This house is hell - no, hell is this house,
Devils run and Satan hides.
If you dare, your soul will die,
There's no escape,
One must live and the other must die.
It's grey outside, it's grey inside me,
He killed my soul; he tightens the walls,
He wants my blood - I don't know why!
I want to know why he wants to reap my soul,
It's like a pirate after his precious treasure.
The clocks tick as seconds pass by,
My blood is dripping.
Silently gushing out,
Someone, please get me out!

Marcel Mieszkowski (10)
St Matthew's Primary School, Luton

The Doll's House

Lucy's eyes were eerily black,
Macy's eyes were cold and cracked.
In the house this meant nothing,
For a doll's eyes were always cunning.

Harriet's smile was sad and torn,
Sunny's smile was fake and looked down,
In the house this meant nothing,
For a doll's smile was never stunning.

But when Hannah used to play,
Their smile lit up the whole day!
We don't talk about Hannah anymore,
And that is all Bella's fault.

The sky was like an inky sea,
With glowing fish swimming freely,
Bella returned, her hands all red,
"I did ask nicely," she said silently,
After we heard a slash from Hannah's bed.

Marilia Maxhari (11)
St Matthew's Primary School, Luton

The Deep Dark Woods

The lightning and thunder made bangs as the
black car sped up.
The car, black as pitch, broke down with me inside.
Surrounded by tall, sinister trees in the deep dark
woods.
I stood outside the car.

The car started to hiss.
Hearing croaky whispers chanting.
I was startled, trying to get over it.
Mysteriously, I heard a horn groan louder than the
lightning.

Petrified, trying to open the car door,
I realised it was locked.
My heavy breathing filled the air,
For I felt like someone was there.

The voice of a man groaning I could hear.
Looking behind me, suddenly appeared
Distinctive handwriting
Saying, 'You shall disappear'.

Jaydon West (11)
St Matthew's Primary School, Luton

Serial Killer

As the silence stretched out into the air,
I moved, feeling beautifully disgusted.
Bang! The bang was as loud as a bass drum.
Whispering echoes were like silent screams.
A frightening killer, a trap had been planned.
I couldn't chase him but he could chase me,
He could destroy me but I couldn't destroy him.
I. Am. Dead...
I had to get out, but how?
There was only one way.
Fighting the serial killer,
I took a bat and was ready to kill him, once and for all.
As I saw him I thought I would die.
He was covered in red,
Covered in devils!
I attacked, *boom!*
He was way too powerful.

Zakariyya Malik (10)
St Matthew's Primary School, Luton

Whispers

Do you hear the restless souls?
Their skin as pale as snow,
Flying down the hall without a sound,
When you hear them you have been found.

Do not listen to their desperate wails,
For once you've heard a sinful spectre,
You shan't hide from them now,
For you have been spotted, you have been found.

When they step forward, do not flinch,
When they grasp you, do not quinch,
The heavy lightness on your back,
Do not move for you have been found.

The deafening silence pins you down,
The curious walls will stop and stare,
For when the wandering spirits come out,
You will be noticed, you will be found.

Natalia Wroblewska (11)
St Matthew's Primary School, Luton

The Deadly Walk

Drip, drip, drip, the rain trickles down like silent tears.
Trees whisper truth and lies.
The manipulating moon puts on a wicked smile, ready to rule death and darkness.
A shadow follows it, ready to commit a crime - murder.
Its deadly glare could melt a thousand souls.
Aargh!
A blood-curdling scream shoots through the air.
Shriek! Shriek!
Bats come out at night - never to return.
As death envelops me, the terrified spirits cry a venomous river.
Slowly, the river awakens devouring everything in its way!
Drip, drip, drip, a dark figure comes closer and closer, whispering like death...

Rebecca Grab (10)
St Matthew's Primary School, Luton

Death Is Following Me

Death is following my steps
Footsteps are near me and I hear a screech
Somebody is behind me, who is it though?
Death shape-shifts into my biggest fear
Big eyes and large spikes growing out of the back
The wind howls like a pack of hungry wolves
Lightning strikes down on a tree
Burning the lies that many have told
Death launches into me, asking my name
Making my heart freeze in fear
My name isn't told as I ignore my fear
Death roars in anger and mocks my steps
Can't they hear my silent screams?
Death follows me...
But when I glare back
Death is gone...
Daylight has taken back control.

Aleksandra Janewa (11)
St Matthew's Primary School, Luton

The Curse Of The Well

Around the well there lies a curse
That can't be fixed by a nurse
Inside the well has bones and a skull
But you can barely see as it is so dull

The curse is not a legend nor a myth
And it is definitely not a gift
No one would go near the well
But not the guy that fell
Death will be staring into your eyes
So make sure you keep that in mind

The curse will give people a fright
Especially in the dead of night
People won't recognise you
They'll just think you're ink or goo

You won't want to know what it'll do
So in short it will be the terrible doom of you!

Abdur-Rahman Brora (11)
St Matthew's Primary School, Luton

The Forest At Midnight

Tall trees above me like deadly giants,
Whispering echoes were like silent screams.
Twigs were snapping under my feet,
As dark shadows lurked behind the trees.
Drops of rain started to trickle down,
Whilst the heavy wind whooshed through the air.
The terrified moon lit up the path,
As giant trees danced in the wind.
Eerie voices were following me.
With every step I took, another formed behind me,
The toxic smell of death filled the air,
As thunder roared.
Suddenly silence, everything stopped.
No more voices, no more shadows.
It felt like someone special had happened,
As daytime came to visit.

Ferdous Kabiri (11)
St Matthew's Primary School, Luton

Murder Mystery

Creeping through the bushes was a soul trying
to escape,
While new victims await.
The smell of death was near,
As a black silhouette started to appear.
The beginning was not too far away since death
was near.

The darkness was like a blanket covering the
night sky,
While an evil presence was close by.
A life-threatening scream filled the air,
Now they were all alone, starting to care,
Finding dead bodies everywhere!

Falling for traps and ending up dead,
Their souls maybe could have been spared.
Still on the search, the murderer hasn't been
found,
While new victims await.

Grace Yanju (10)
St Matthew's Primary School, Luton

Is Someone Following?

Sinister shadows of the night lurking behind,
Am I going crazy? Are they alive?
Howling wind like a whole wolf pack.
It's coming after me, will I survive?

Sinister shadows of the night lurking behind,
Something flickering in the distance I find.
A black candle of night still alight.
Should I take it?

Sinister shadows of the night lurking behind,
Branches are daggers coming to fight.
Cracking leaves and shrieks fill the night.

Sinister shadows of the night lurking behind,
If I could, I'd cry a river, sadly I
Can't, for I'm a living spectre.

Kamila Kotlinska (10)
St Matthew's Primary School, Luton

The Nightmare Side

The terrified moon hid behind the dark clouds.
Tall towering trees stood like silent soldiers.
Crows croaked loudly, snatching souls of innocent people.
Dark shadows danced menacingly around me.

Silent screams pierced the forest like ravens screeching.
Endless thunder roared violently through the forest.
Vines twisted around the old tree like snakes.
The icy wind whispered quietly through the darkness.

Angry wolves howled in the distance,
Loud enough to be heard around the world.
Bushes rustled even when there was no wind.
The crow swooped past me as quick as a flash.

Malaika Lodhi (11)
St Matthew's Primary School, Luton

The Forest

Entering the forest through the crumbling arch,
You get an eerie feeling.
Tall, skinny trees envelop the star-soaked sky,
Walking through the forest,
You see bones scattered across the ground.

Walking further in the forest,
The wind gets stronger.
You hear a distant crunch
And your heartbeat gets louder.

Running further into the forest,
Silence decides to stretch out.
It's soon broken by the whistles of trains.

A distinctive sound of sirens wailing fills the
atmosphere.
Your blood runs cold,
You decide to run further, sealing your fate.

Ada Gubas (11)
St Matthew's Primary School, Luton

The Hidden Haunted House

In the hidden haunted house,
Spider silk spawns creepy cobwebs
To catch their flying prey,
Making sure nothing remains.

In the hidden haunted house,
The silent screams don't shake the deafening
silence
As dark shadows weep and yelp for help
Forever waiting to be freed from their hell.

In the hidden haunted house,
The tall trees nearby wait patiently,
For travellers nearby to be claimed by their lies
Then they go back to waiting to claim more lives.

In the hidden haunted house
Mysteries lie, never to be solved...

Keelan Devlin (11)
St Matthew's Primary School, Luton

Play Time

This day was monstrous.
I was dealing with kids in a play area,
But it was a 24-hour shift.
So I had to stay till night.
It was time for the children to go but they stayed,
No parents in sight.

I should have resigned because what happened tonight,
Was a frightful bang.
I was trying to do something but it caught my eye.

It was as dark as space then it hit me.
It was a tentacle of a squid.
It pulled all the children to the ball pit.
It was slimy - it was big but it stared at me.
I anxiously awaited.
My blood ran cold.

Fazal Waseem (10)
St Matthew's Primary School, Luton

The Louder The More Silent It Was

Drip, drip, drip, trickled down the blood,
As shadows danced through the dark, deadly night,
I was filled with horror and fright,
Darkness swept all over the house so I hid like a little mouse.

Drip, drip, drip, trickled down the blood,
The thunder roared with all its might,
I was filled with horror and fright,
There goes my sleep, it's walking away.

Drip, drip, drip, trickled down the blood,
My candle had lost its light,
I was filled with horror and fright,
Then suddenly silence consumed the night.

Arabella McIntyre (11)
St Matthew's Primary School, Luton

Ring Around The Rosie

Ring around the Rosie,
A body, a body, we all fall to death.
I walk down the dishevelled death road but then
"La la la la la!"
A little girl starts singing.
And at that moment is when the impossible
becomes possible.
My heart is beating as fast as a light can go on
and off.
Scratching noises, footsteps as loud as a car can
go rev.
Bushes going crash together.
Lightning strikes the ground.
I can hear the song again.
Ring around the Rosie.
But this time I can
Hear it closer and closer.
And this is my last words. Uh oh.

Ricardo Nambam Sanha (10)
St Matthew's Primary School, Luton

Endless Scream

E ndless screams are coming my way

N ever look back - it's too late

"D ie," says a voice behind me

L ightning shoots down like deadly daggers

E veryone stops for a moment

S ilence is here - all the trees are whispering about me

S teps are coming towards me

S hadows are peering through doors

C reaks are getting louder

R un or he will get you

E ndless thoughts run through my head

A im for the door - run now!

M inutes go by, now I am gone...

Aleesa Afzal (10)
St Matthew's Primary School, Luton

Alone At Midnight

The old door creaked menacingly as I entered the
house
The abandoned house was filled with darkness
My heart started pounding
As endless screams pierced through the silence

Floorboards groaned as I went upstairs
The cracked window shattered into pieces
But I still continued trying to escape
When I looked back there was a shadow

Sinister shadows danced menacingly all around me
Fear shook down my spine
So I hid in a room
Silently holding my breath

Still hiding from the strange shadows
But then it caught me.

Deken Walsh (10)
St Matthew's Primary School, Luton

The Dark Figure

Mesmerising moonlight shines into my room,
Like a deadly torch leading to doom.
I try to reach safety,
In an attempt to escape the cruelty!

Shadows lurk everywhere,
Creaks and cracks here and there.
All of a sudden, a deafening silence,
As I watch the tree branches pointing with
violence.

I now realise I am not alone.
A figure as dark as the night sky stands and
stomps around me,
My heart is a beating drum.
I have never known until now,

That I slowly have morphed into the dark figure
himself...

Dannah Sunish (11)
St Matthew's Primary School, Luton

The Last Of My Soul

I approached the gothic land,
As I began to feel a mother's hand.
I heard a whoosh and whoo,
Oh, how I wish I was with a crew.
My fear felt like cold fire,
Seemed like the person who told me about this
place was a liar.

I came closer to the haunted house,
Later, I saw an infectious mouse.
I saw the trees waving at me,
Now I felt like I wanted to pee.

The house door opened on its own,
After, I heard the ring of a telephone.
The ghosts took me away,
And my last words were, "Hey!"

Rehan Syed (11)
St Matthew's Primary School, Luton

Job Nightmare

I should have stuck to cleaning,
But I got a feeling.
I heard loud whispers.
I tried to ignore it,
But the lights went out.
It was pitch-black, I tried to stay back.

I should have stuck to cleaning,
But I never knew I was stealing.
I dropped my broom and cautiously crept to the
other room,
Bang! I knew it would be soon.

I should have stuck to cleaning,
But now I'm silently screaming.
The freezer was as cold as the North Pole,
Now I know what I stole.
This was when I froze.

Zofia Sabiniarz (10)
St Matthew's Primary School, Luton

The Gentle Caress

I close my eyes, getting some shut-eye,
Surely knowing there's no one nearby.
All of a sudden I feel someone caress my neck,
I silently scream and become a nervous wreck.

As quick as a flash, my nerves kick in,
I break my window and fall in the bin.
The wind whistles, I start to run,
Thinking that this is no fun.

Flash! I'm in the deep, dark forest, lightning
chuckles,
I look down at my shoe and fix my buckles.
I stop for a while and come to find,
Something lurking from behind...

Jadesola Adeshina (11)
St Matthew's Primary School, Luton

Living In An Isolated Manor

Deep within the shadows,
There lies dormant souls.
Through all their time without any liver,
Surely they must have cried a river.

Deep within the shadows,
The living dead approaches again.
Trapped within like mice,
They will love to scream twice.

Deep within the shadows,
The floorboards crack like backs.
A distant door starts creaking,
Bang! The darkness continues crawling in.

Deep within the shadows,
These are mystical moments before I disappear
forever.

Bradley Siluba (11)
St Matthew's Primary School, Luton

The Marathon

As my heart beats like a drum
As I run I am numb
Because I chose to run
Every day of every minute of every second it's
me and my gun

Up to the centre and across the roads
While I go up to the dangerous holes
While I swim through the lake making *splash,
splash, splash*
My friend Mich thought he could make it, he
was wrong

As the moon shines in my eyes
While everyone I see dies with lies
But then I see it so I run and run
Until I say hello to death that night.

Szymon Chris Sniec (11)
St Matthew's Primary School, Luton

The Mysterious Creature Of Darkness

My head was weak yet I went high into the clouds,
My jaw was open and I was screaming mumbled
words until everything went black.

I tried to remember it lying on the floor,
But thinking about it made me tremble even more.

As I heard the wolves howling and the water of
rain dripping down,
I felt something dark and it didn't want to drain
away.

I remembered seeing movements and hearing
tapping on the window,
But when I turned around I saw something
unimaginable
That I will never forget.

Destiny-Marie Fowler (11)
St Matthew's Primary School, Luton

House Of Horror

Lilly entered the house
She heard faint screaming but couldn't turn back
She heard distant footsteps from behind her back

As she entered the room
She heard a witch cackling on her broom
Screaming in pain with blood in her veins

A frantic night full of fright
Silent screams from kids in daydreams
As the bright light flickered appeared a mysterious
figure

Silent whispers from all the pictures
She looked at the shadows, the shadows looked
back
She couldn't turn back.

Amelia Rowley (10)
St Matthew's Primary School, Luton

In The Gloomy Forest

In the gloomy forest,
The spine-chilling spirits lurk behind the towering trees
Taking souls of abandoned children.

In the gloomy forest,
The trees' branches point like deadly daggers in the night
Terminating anyone who dares to come close.

In the gloomy forest,
The luminous moon silently tiptoes behind a dull cloud
Terrified of the vibrations from the spirits' screams.

In the gloomy forest,
A sinister silhouette stands behind me with a knife...
Is this the end?

Siyana Sultana (10)
St Matthew's Primary School, Luton

World's Haunted House

Hard rain - it happens every day,
The window screams again and again,
This is intense,
This does not make sense.

Floorboards creak on repeat,
This is something my head has to compete.
Why me though?
This is definitely not okay.

Light flickers all about,
It gives me no doubts.
The star-soaked skies give me all the light,
No hope is found in the starry night.

My music box plays about,
This is not what I planned out.
I wish that I was making this up.

Julia Gluzinska (10)
St Matthew's Primary School, Luton

The Room

As I walked around the room
My eyes started to bloom
Staring around petrified as could be
The frightening noise made me scream!

My eyes were like a hawk trying to find
But nothing close, maybe it climbed
Climbing up but nothing to catch clean
But talk too soon, I would be seen

With the last minutes of my life
I caught my breath and went twice
Glimpsing around the room
I got caught and died too soon
If you ever go to this place
Always remember this case.

Athil Ali (11)
St Matthew's Primary School, Luton

The Vicious Hyde

As I strode past the clueless Hyde,
Into the deep dark forest,
They crumpled in my zone,
It was a graveyard full of bones,
Then I stumbled upon the tallest.

The house screamed in pain,
The darkness was a veil,
Then the bell started to bail,
It started to expel,
My heart became a cold cell.

Cautiously creeping,
Hyde was already seeking,
I think I turned pale,
My skin colour the same as a nail,
He was laughing in the clear just the second I
disappeared.

Bartosz Smielecki (11)
St Matthew's Primary School, Luton

The Car Child

I hear a loud crash
I turn my head as quick as a flash
Here I am on the ground
With smiling trees all around
The trees go far and far
In the distance there's a car
Around the car there's moss
I wonder how much it will cost
But there's a little shadow on the path
It starts to laugh
I look back at the car
And it drives far and far
I wonder what's going on
But the child is gone
The child and the car disappear
All my memories are fears.

Enrika Mihada (11)
St Matthew's Primary School, Luton

The Clock Strikes Midnight

At the haunted house,
Midnight struck.
Ghoulish ghosts started peering around
As the hushed whispers turned into deadly echoes.

Endless echoes came towards me,
Couldn't look back, it was too late.
"Surrender," a whisper said beside me.
My heart started racing.

At the haunted house,
Lights started flickering like deadly shadows,
Trees stood tall like deadly daggers,
Deafening silence filled the room
Hoping all this destruction stops.

Nathaniel Mwanza (11)
St Matthew's Primary School, Luton

Empty Room

At midnight, you're all alone,
The light flickers on its own.
The rain like thunder growls and groans,
Hollow sounds come from the ground.
Cautious silence fills the air.
The house screams in pain,
Be careful because you're about to faint.

Tick-tock, time is on the clock,
The bird is about to mock.
Look out from the sky,
It's all full of lies.
Don't sigh, you won't be fine.
Clangs and clatters,
it will get better.

Elle Yit (11)
St Matthew's Primary School, Luton

Shivers

I carefully went onto the boat
I needed to go home,
But I needed time.
It was like I had a warning
Halfway there I stopped.
The wind was roaring,
Then suddenly there was silent screaming.
Rain started to pour heavily.
I guess I'd have to wait until the morning.
This was getting out of hand.
I was sleeping,
The silence stretched out.
I woke up,
My heavy breathing filled the air.
I finally got to the end,
Then I was never seen again.

Siele Antanaviciute (11)
St Matthew's Primary School, Luton

The Forest

As they walked through the forest
A new place to explore
Far away land so ominous and eerie
A night sky was like an inky sea
With luminescent fish swimming inside it.

As they walked through the forest
With trees like daggers looming
Over them it was a cobweb in the sky
Hoot hoot, they could hear the echo from the owls
above.

As they walked through the forest
With fear in their bodies
No one out looking for them
What will they do...?

Deenah Halimi (10)
St Matthew's Primary School, Luton

The Chase Of Death

Deafening silence fills the air
Make a noise, I would not dare
I'm running at an even pace
Begging I don't meet it face to face

Meeting a spirit like this is so very rare
This chase is clearly not fair
My heart aches
As I reflect on my mistakes
I'll try and find another path
Praying I don't face its wrath

I'll try to run
This really isn't fun
I can hear its subtle breaths
Tonight I might greet death...

Chloe Mcguiness (10)
St Matthew's Primary School, Luton

The Deathly Spirit

Roses are red, violets are blue,
Why do you sense someone stalking you?
Even when you sleep you see lights are flickering
And shadows of death sitting next to you.
When you tremble in fear the spirit likes it
But if you keep calm it won't trouble you.
If you suddenly decide to go somewhere to get
peace and quiet
The ghost will follow your footsteps.
When you're alone there is no one and
Nothing can save you because the ghost might
kill you.

Joseph Oche Igoche (11)
St Matthew's Primary School, Luton

The Shadows Of The Room

At the back of the room,
A shadow stands.
Gazing into deep eyes,
Unknown, silent stance.
Fear floods the room,
As the figure knocks: *tap, tap,*
Waking him up,
With a fearful fright,
Searching for a glimpse of movement,
Like a snake the shadow slithers,
Waiting for its guest to come into a mindful trance.
At the back of the room,
The shadow now stands,
In open air, their eyes connect,
Now trapped in a stance of despair.

Dwight Acquah (11)
St Matthew's Primary School, Luton

The Frightening House In The Eerie Night

The frightening house in the eerie night,
Within flickering lights,
Dark shadows lurking at midnight,
I have to choose life or death.

Choosing to live,
I dare to go in,
Inside this haunted house,
Where I can't escape.

Going closer,
Inside the frightening house,
Looking around,
Where could it be?

I look behind myself,
And finally find it.
I run towards it
But instantly regret it.

Zuzanna Nawvocka (11)
St Matthew's Primary School, Luton

The Mystery Mirror

The mirror is hanging
Upon the deadly, dangerous wall it shines
Let it rip, let it die

A crack in the window
A crack in the sky
The world is perfect
But everything dies inside

It enters through the blinding light
Like a diamond in the sky
It will haunt you throughout the day and night
While it exits through the shivering light
The ghouls seem gone
But something remains
Something gets left behind.

Medeea Droga (11)
St Matthew's Primary School, Luton

The Haunted House

It was late at night
And there was moonlight,
Then suddenly a thunderstorm came.
I ran into a haunted house while it rained dogs and
cats outside.

I went in and to my surprise, I saw spirits,
They were white as fog.
The house made a silent scream,
As I saw star-soaked skies.

I summoned up all my courage to the bedroom,
It was filled with dolls.
Then scary moonlight came
And a frantic scream.

Khalid Atunrase (11)
St Matthew's Primary School, Luton

Deep, Dark Woods

Walking through the dark forest
The wind whispers
All of a sudden there are wolves howling in the
distance
With a glow of lightning that lights up
As quick as a flash in the night sky.

Don't be scared of the night
There are always bad sights
There just has to be light in the deep, dark woods
The shadows stare back as they whisper about you
Blood runs cold as the spirits cautiously creep
towards you.

Gabriel Kotecki (11)
St Matthew's Primary School, Luton

What Happens In The Middle Of The Night

In the dead of the night,
You might want to hide,
Because if you don't,
It will make you cry.

In the dead of the night,
It will want you to die.
If you could hear the door creak open,
You will know your house is haunted.

In the dead of the night,
You will hear blood-curdling screams,
Like deadly daggers piercing the night,
And that's what happens in the middle of
the night.

Nikola Banach (10)
St Matthew's Primary School, Luton

Ghost Invasion

The rain splashes on the floor
With shadows running around you
Distant howling echoes like
A heart-stopping horror film.

Thunder rumbles like
Deadly lions
The windows crack when lightning shines.

The moon is the only thing
Lighting up the forest
Suddenly I hear creepy music
And silent footsteps walking towards me.

Death is following me everywhere...

Kacper Falkowski (11)
St Matthew's Primary School, Luton

The Dark Shed

Silent screaming
And heavy breathing

Now it suddenly all makes sense
Wow, this is quite intense

Help, seriously, I need help
Screaming and shouting will not help

This is really scary, I'm not going to lie
But honestly, this is wasting my time

This is getting out of hand
But I did not pay attention
Because my feet are killing me.

Ava Jaklik-Street (11)
St Matthew's Primary School, Luton

Space

There was no air nor light,
The silence stretched out,
I couldn't breathe,
My heart was a beating drum,
The wind whispered to me,
The stars cautiously crept around me.

The darkness killed me,
I was alone,
Not another soul around me,
The darkness was a veil as my blood ran cold,
The endless tune of silence bore me,
I had sealed my own fate.

Oluwatomisin Taiwo (10)
St Matthew's Primary School, Luton

The Abandoned House

Crack goes the floor
As I open the door
A scream is heard
So a lesson is learnt
I turn left
Reminding myself
I'm in the old abandoned house
I hide like a little mouse

Splash! The rain falls
From the dark sky
As the deadly bats begin to fly
A howling scream seems
To be near me
I hope no one sees me!

Denis Leleu (11)
St Matthew's Primary School, Luton

Deserted

In the deserted, demolished church
Lots of things broken
All damaged
Left like that
No one to clean this mess

Dirty and dusty
Left alone
No one to investigate what happened
Or who did this
A disturbing noise coming from not far
A black figure haunting the place

A hidden man who holds a secret
With a mysterious face.

Conor Morsley-Gavin (11)
St Matthew's Primary School, Luton

My Fate

The darkness around me was an impenetrable veil.
Roar, the rushing wind was like hail,
As soon as I stepped in, I sealed my fate.

The stars soaked the skies,
The crescent moon rose.
As dark as night, my blood ran cold.

As the stars looked over me,
I lay down and closed my eyes,
Under the starry sky,
I sealed my fate.

Ziqi Liu (11)
St Matthew's Primary School, Luton

The Darkness Was A Veil

The darkness was a veil,
My blood ran cold.
Distressed, I waited,
As silent screams were heard.

The darkness was a veil,
In the shadow I shall hide.
The moon rose up,
In the star-soaked sky.

The darkness was a veil.
The headstone watched;
The shadows stared back,
I turned around but I never looked back...

Tazrian Ahmed (11)
St Matthew's Primary School, Luton

In The Night

In the night there's fright upon the moonlight
Bats and rats give away frights
And the dead awaken in the scary night.

In the night the light shines bright with all your
might
Just for one fright, the midnight towers over towns
Children cry over the candy, the vampires come
out of hiding
All in the scary night.

Owen Brackstone (11)
St Matthew's Primary School, Luton

The Walk In The House

Silent screaming,
Heavy breathing,
Children weeping,
Cautiously creeping.

The house screamed in pain,
It was as loud as a bass drum,
Shadows laughed at me,
My blood ran cold.

The wind whispered,
There was a crunch underneath my feet,
Now it all makes sense,
It is all complete.

Irfan Ahmed (11)
St Matthew's Primary School, Luton

In A Horror House

You are in a dark house
Silent screams are around
Shadows are behind you
It is too late
Don't look at it!
The door is creaking in the wind

The electricity is off
Darkness hiding the house
Sometimes we walk at night all alone
He follows me home
Sometimes he speaks in mumbled tones.

Keivin Hasaj (11)
St Matthew's Primary School, Luton

Death

In the dark night,
Silent whispers gave me a fright.
Thunder and lightning in the woods,
That gave me a terrified feeling of danger.

My heart was a beating drum,
My heavy breathing filled the air like smoke.
My head was screaming for help.
Until I looked down I knew I was dead...

Sahil Miah (10)
St Matthew's Primary School, Luton

The Only Eye

The breathing sky, opening the dark night,
Near the blue, over the loo,
You will see people watching you,
After all, the wall will be seen by many different
signs.
Shadows like to be around or even fly to stay alive.
The countless hours, the overtime,
People are dying, and so are you.

Julia Dabrowksa (11)
St Matthew's Primary School, Luton

Francis' Story

It was black as coal,
She was wide awake
Ready to make an escape.

The wind hideously howled
While she paddled away.
Out of nowhere, there was a noise.

Knock.
Since that day she was never seen
But a message was left
'I did knock first'.

Beatrix Kerekes (11)
St Matthew's Primary School, Luton

The Forest

The forest was dark like the night sky,
In the forest there was screaming,
They tried their best to ignore it,
Scared.

The forest trees were as tall as a building,
In the forest there was a broken well,
They tried to see what was in it,
Splash.

Kamil Babusa (11)
St Matthew's Primary School, Luton

Deadly

D oor creaking loudly
E scape the deadly shadow
A bandoned house stands alone
D anger all around
L urking shadow behind me
Y elling voice from the darkness.

Scarlett Maccow (10)
St Matthew's Primary School, Luton

Spirit

A ghostly ghost, is it a joke?
You could say it is terrifying or scary.

You could try to be its friend
But not its enemy.

It will haunt you
Scare you with whispers...

Maame Afia (10)
St Matthew's Primary School, Luton

Summer

Plants are pretty, can't you see?
But in summertime, they're as pretty as can be.
When you are walking or having a stroll,
You might see someone with a flower they stole.
A plant you can often see are daisies,
And to that, no one has an excuse to be lazy!

In summertime, it is cool
To see that a lot of people have a pool.
To add to that, you can eat a tangerine
Or even play on your trampoline.

Now it is summer we can go on the field
And I think everyone will be appealed.
There are loads of games you can play
Or you can just go on the boat
Or just act like a goat!

Annalise Sharpe (10)
Stanton Community Primary School, Stanton

Hidden Wonders

The dazzling light blue sea sparkles as the sun
shines on it.
As the soft sandy beaches fade into the clear aqua
sea,
The wonderful creatures swim and splash in the
pearlescent sea.
From above, it's like seeing azure blue diamonds
twinkling like the stars.
But it's like there is a different world down in the
great deep.
More beautiful than you could ever imagine.
It carries amazing myths.
There are wonderful secrets ready to be found
And lost cities underground.
For here is a poem of a glorious world.

Seren Olney (11)
Stanton Community Primary School, Stanton

An Enchanting Night

The vast sky is wearing her regal, ebony gown
And her faceless moon is smiling delightfully in its
form of a crescent.
The crystalised rhinestone stars show no sign of a
frown
As the meandering stretch of fresh air coils around
the luminescence.

The ring of the vivid solar system is churning
As the wind pulls the night along by a single air
thread
Slowly but surely, the last of the night is burning
As many youths and elders are sleeping deeply in
their comfortable beds.

Abigail Mayes (11)
Stanton Community Primary School, Stanton

Help The Environment

Trees help us,
But we go on a bus,
That does nothing,
We're acting like our planet isn't a thing,
I think we should stop taking this for granted!
Look how much we've planted!
Do you really want to stop now?
After we've done, let's take a bow!
We need to help the trees!
We need to help the bees!
We need to help everything!
We're acting like a broken wing!

Holly Maudlin-Moss (9)
Stanton Community Primary School, Stanton

Flower Passion

Love the way you smell so sweet,
Love your scent, it's like sweet perfume,
Love you because you are a beautiful treat,
Love you because you amaze my eyes when
you bloom,
Love it when bees take your nectar to eat,
Love your colours, they take away the gloom,
Love your petals, they are so neat,
Love the way you excite me and make my heart
go boom!

Isabelle Steed (8)
Stanton Community Primary School, Stanton

Sunny Day

Sun, oh sun
It's time to play
Sun, oh sun
Don't go away

Coming outside
The breeze on my knees
My dog by my side
I'm loving the bees

Bees buzzing beautifully
Dancing flowers
Running smoothly
We are loving

Flowers flowing
Daisies dancing
Making every moment beautiful.

Summer Pickup (9)
Stanton Community Primary School, Stanton

RAF Dad

My dad is a soldier
He is so far away
He has been gone since February
But now it's May!
Dad is somewhere very hot
He's in the blazing sun
I really miss him a whole lot
But he will be home soon
He's back in June
That is super soon!

Henry Wright (8)
Stanton Community Primary School, Stanton

Dandelions

As they sway in the wind with their jagged leaves,
They move in the night like midnight thieves,
We cut the beautiful flowers to make some wreaths,
They are so bright that in a fire they still glow,
Even in the flames the fires like to throw.
Dandelions.

Esmie O'Reilly (10)
Stanton Community Primary School, Stanton

Dragon Dreamer

In my dreams I often see a dragon looking down
on me
He has rough scales and a very big tail
The first time I saw him I let out a wail
He looked really weird
But he was not as scary as I feared
Over time I realised he was a disguised spy.

Harry Shaw (8)
Stanton Community Primary School, Stanton

School Is Cool

School is cool,
We play with a ball
Our ball is normally a black ball.

Maths is fun,
Once it's done
We play in the sun.

Caitlin Goodridge (8)
Stanton Community Primary School, Stanton

Singer Of The Night

The wind likes to sing, the birds like to too,
If that's all true then why do we still hear singing
during the rising of the moon?
When the wind goes to bed and the birds sleep on
the sheds,
It is Alulia who sings while the wind and birds rest
their heads.

"Oh, my dear moon, take me away soon
And let me go live with my dear, my moon!
May I soar with elegance and grace,
Oh please someone take my place!"
Alulia called out, she sang and she begged,
That someday she'd be with her moon instead.

But one day a curious child
Came up with an idea so wild.
"Oh, singer of the night, I call on your name,
I have an idea that will not leave you in shame!"
The child called, as Alulia bawled.
"Thank you, what would your name be?"
"Keziah." That child was me.

Shaun Keziah Massengo Fleary (12)
Woodlands Primary School, Linwood

My Hopes And Dreams

I wish I would make everyone happy,
So my wings become very floppy.
My skills at art are very good,
Because it can give me many thrills.
I want to be good in maths,
So I would be the smartest to lead the path.
I want to make many friends,
So there will be many gems.
My dream is to become a YouTuber,
So I would be flush with money.

Anna Maria Reo (12)
Woodlands Primary School, Linwood

The Fairy's Life

Blossoms glitter in the sun
Fairies spread dust during the night run

In the morning the trees swish like tails
And then it's time for the midnight rails.

Teigan Reid (12)
Woodlands Primary School, Linwood

YOUNG WRITERS INFORMATION

We hope you have enjoyed reading this book – and that you will continue to in the coming years.

If you're the parent or family member of an enthusiastic poet or story writer, do visit our website **www.youngwriters.co.uk/subscribe** and sign up to receive news, competitions, writing challenges and tips, activities and much, much more! There's lots to keep budding writers motivated!

If you would like to order further copies of this book, or any of our other titles, then please give us a call or order via your online account.

Young Writers
Remus House
Coltsfoot Drive
Peterborough
PE2 9BF
(01733) 890066
info@youngwriters.co.uk

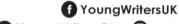
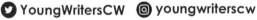

f YoungWritersUK
🐦 YoungWritersCW **📷** youngwriterscw

Scan me to
watch the Poetry
Towers video!